worship
BAND
PLAY-ALONG

DRUMSET EDITION *Volume 3*

How Great Is Our God

T0039907

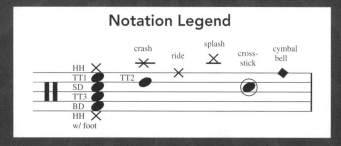

Notation Legend

Recorded and produced by Jim Reith at BeatHouse Music, Milwaukee, WI

Lead Vocals by Tonia Emrich and Jim Reith
Background Vocals by Jim Reith and Janna Wolf
Guitars by Joe Gorman
Bass by Chris Kringel
Keyboard by Kurt Cowling
Drums by Del Bennett

ISBN 978-1-4234-1725-5

HAL•LEONARD®
CORPORATION
7777 W. BLUEMOUND RD. P.O. BOX 13819 MILWAUKEE, WI 53213

Visit Hal Leonard Online at
www.halleonard.com

Above All

Words and Music by Paul Baloche and Lenny LeBlanc

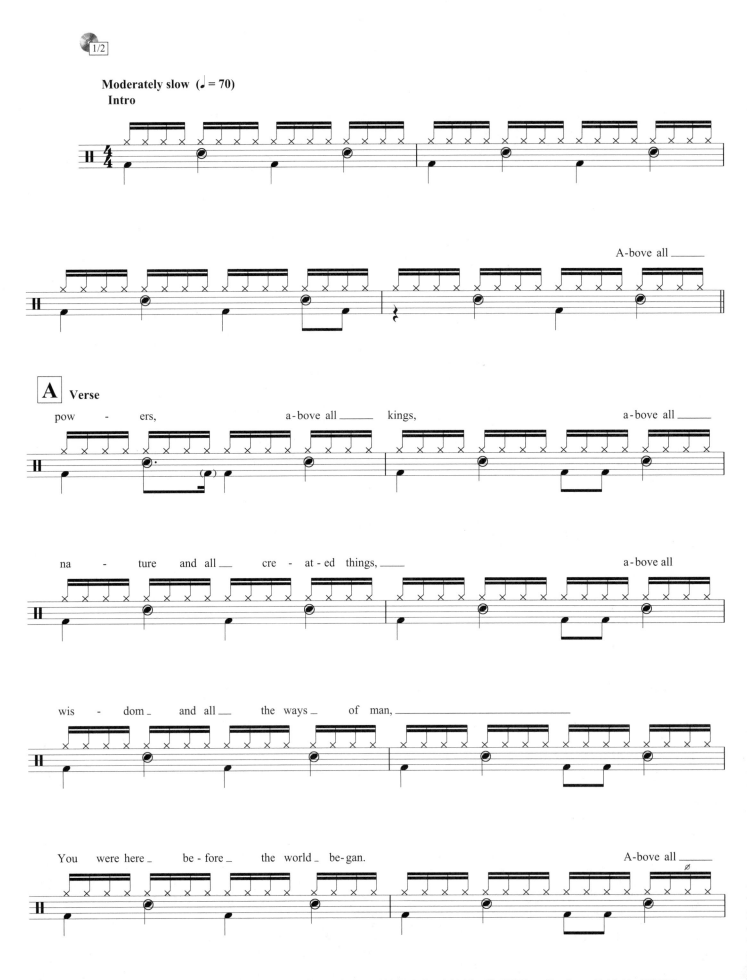

Moderately slow (♩ = 70)
Intro

A-bove all _____

A Verse

pow - ers,   a-bove all _____ kings,   a-bove all _____

na - ture and all _____ cre - at - ed things, _____   a-bove all

wis - dom _ and all _____ the ways _ of man, _____

You were here _ be - fore _ the world _ be - gan.   A-bove all _____

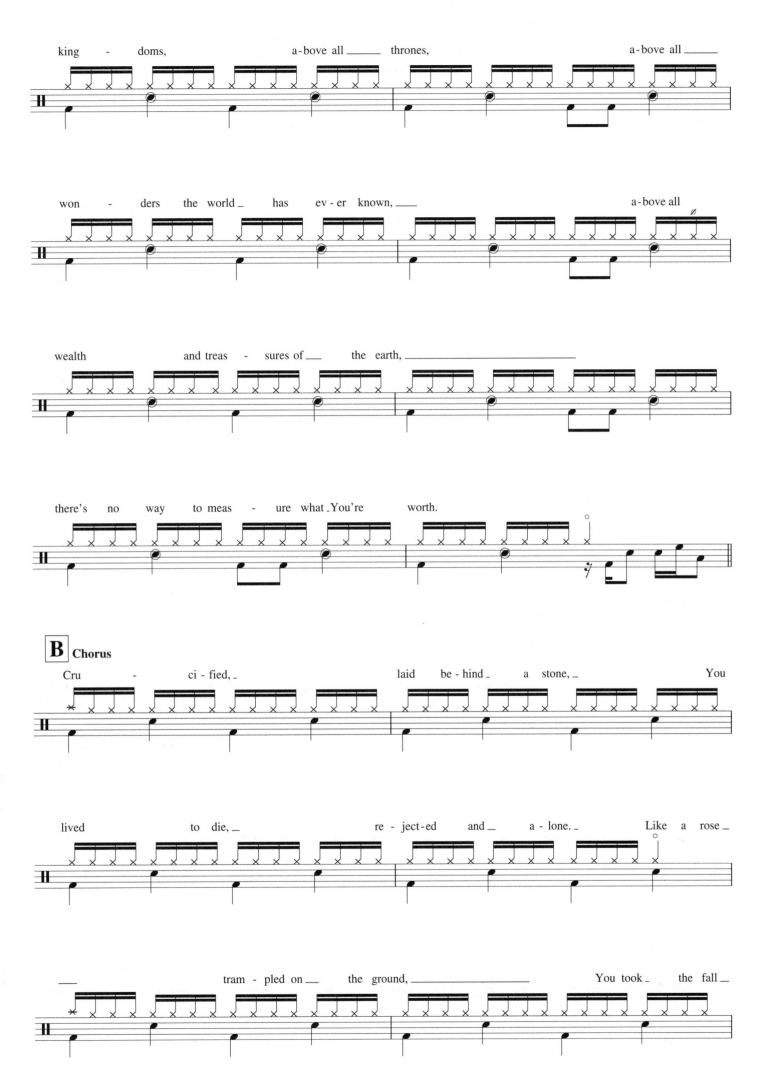

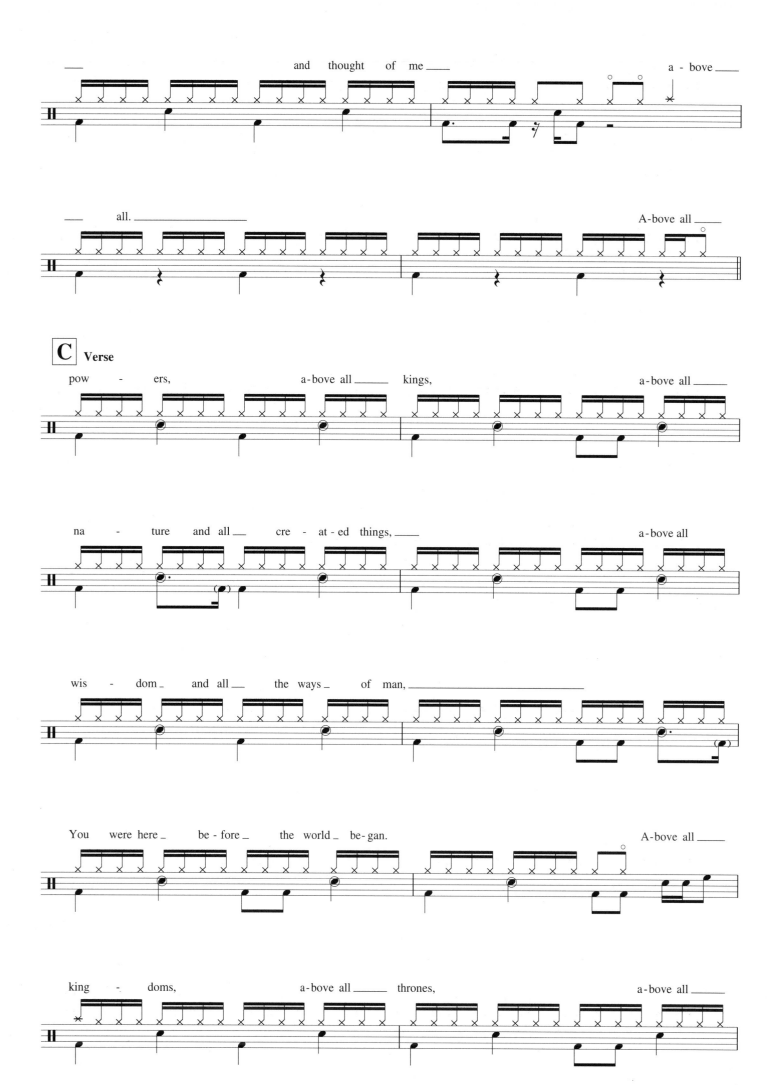

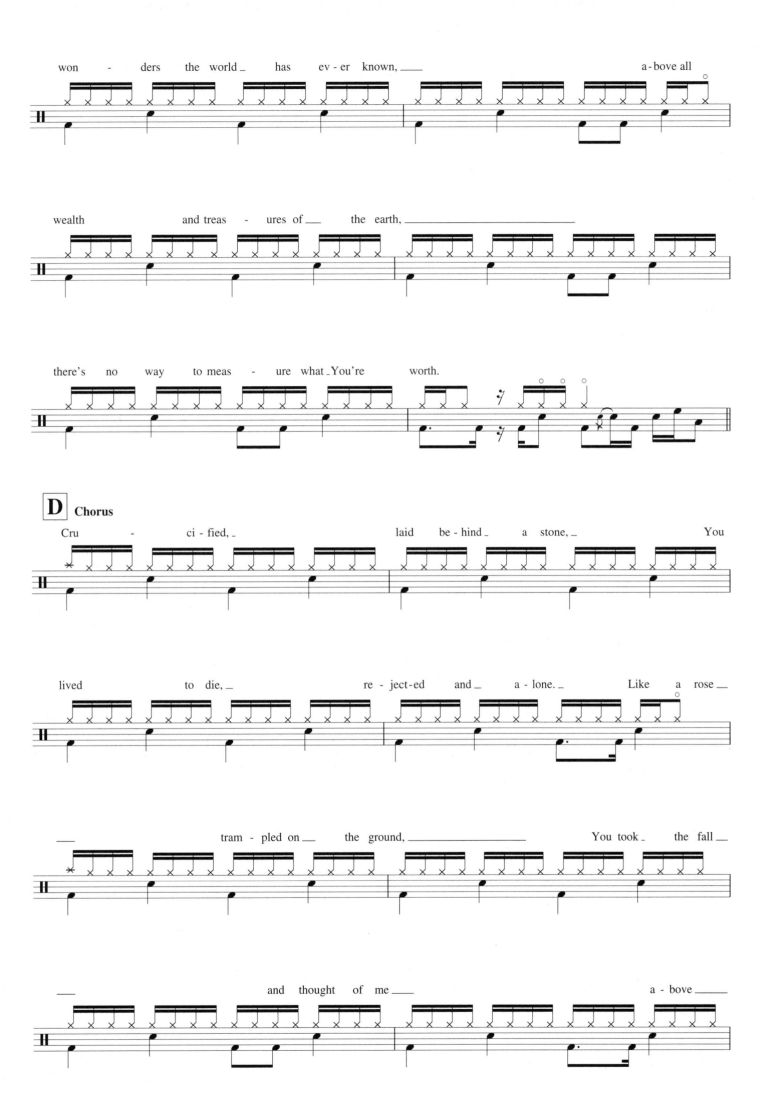

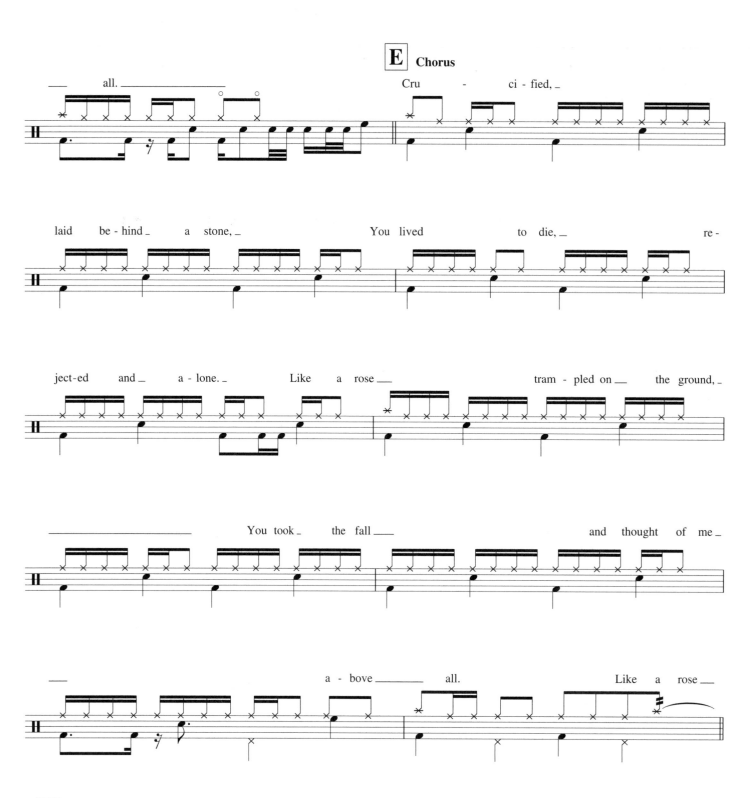

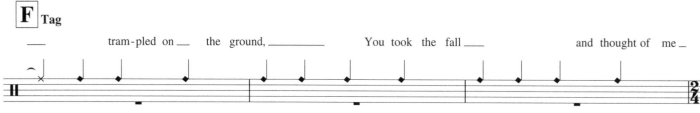

slight rit.

Beautiful Savior
(All My Days)

Words and Music by Stuart Townend

3/4

In a slow 2 (. = ca. 52)
Intro

A **Verse 1**

All _____ my

days I will sing this song of glad - ness,

give _____ my praise to the Foun - tain of de -

lights. For in my _____ help - less - ness, You

heard my _____ cry, and waves of

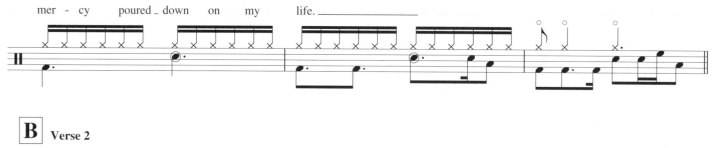

mer - cy poured _ down on my life. _____

B Verse 2

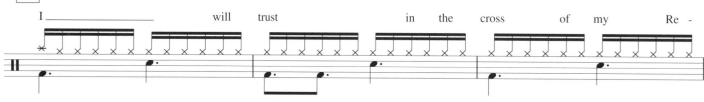

I _____ will trust in the cross of my Re -

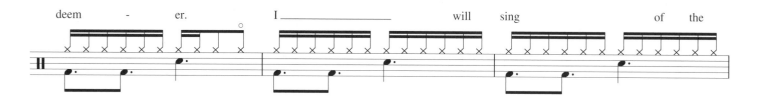

deem - er. I _____ will sing of the

blood that nev - er fails, of sins for -

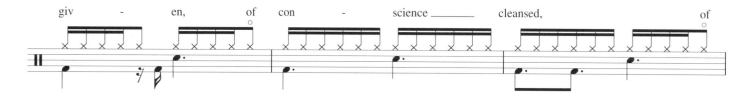

giv - en, of con - science _____ cleansed, of

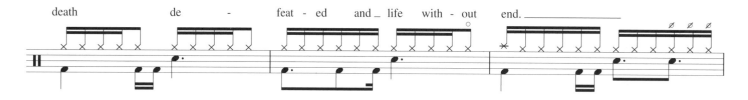

death de - feat - ed and _ life with - out end. _____

C Chorus

Beau - ti - ful Sav - ior, _____ Won - der - ful

Coun - sel - or, clothed in maj - es - ty, Lord of

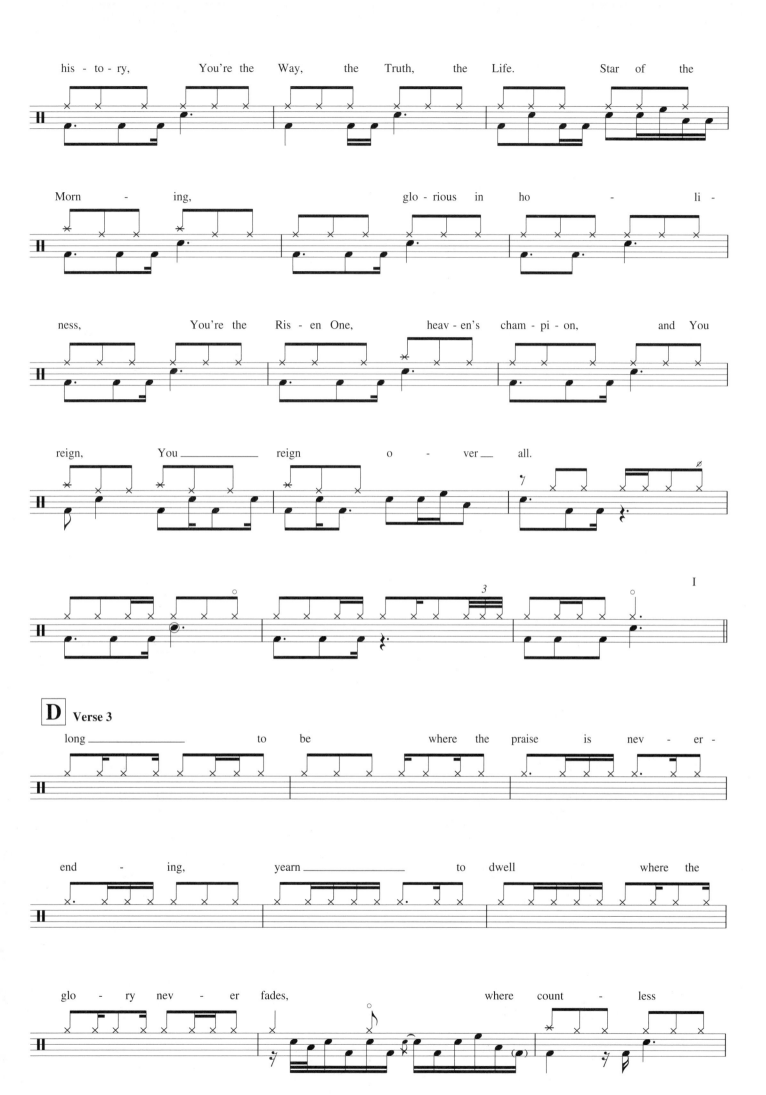

Days of Elijah

Words and Music by Robin Mark

How Great Is Our God

Words and Music by Chris Tomlin, Jesse Reeves and Ed Cash

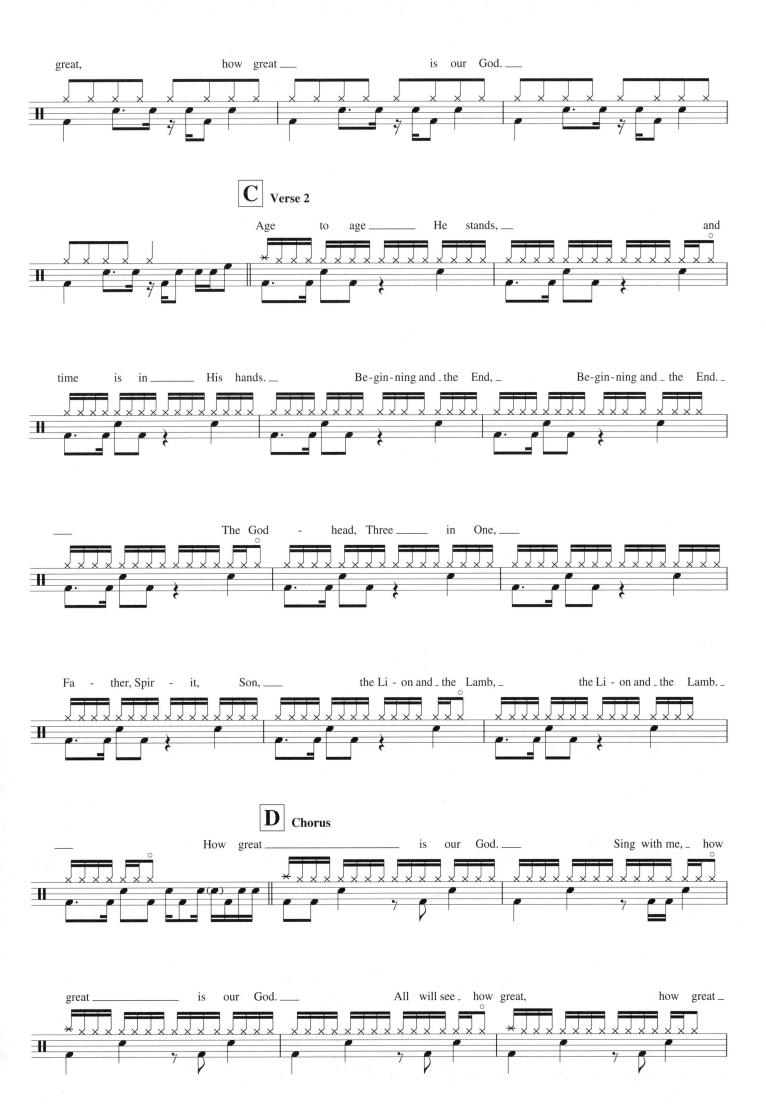

is our God. ___

E **Bridge**

Name a - bove ___ all ___ names, wor - thy of ___ all ___

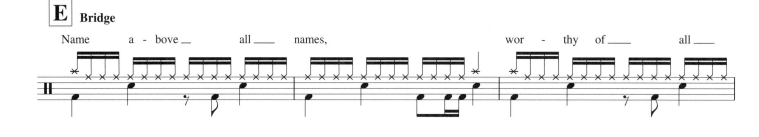

praise. My heart will sing: ___ How great ___ is our God! ___

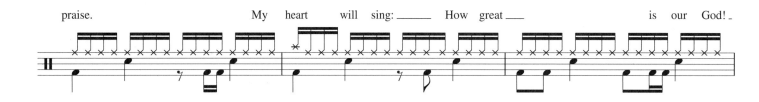

He's the Name a - bove ___ all ___

names, wor - thy of ___ all ___ praise. My

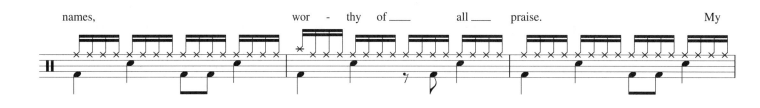

heart will sing: ___ How great ___ is our God! ___

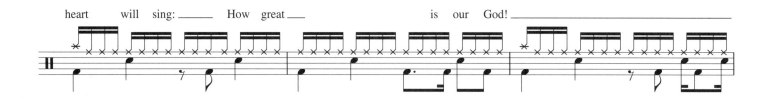

F **Chorus**

___ How great ___ is our God. ___

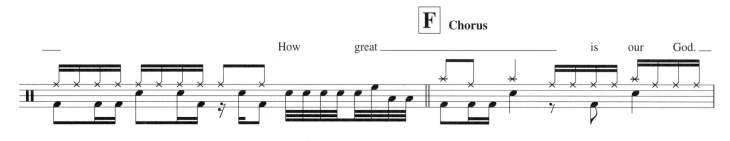

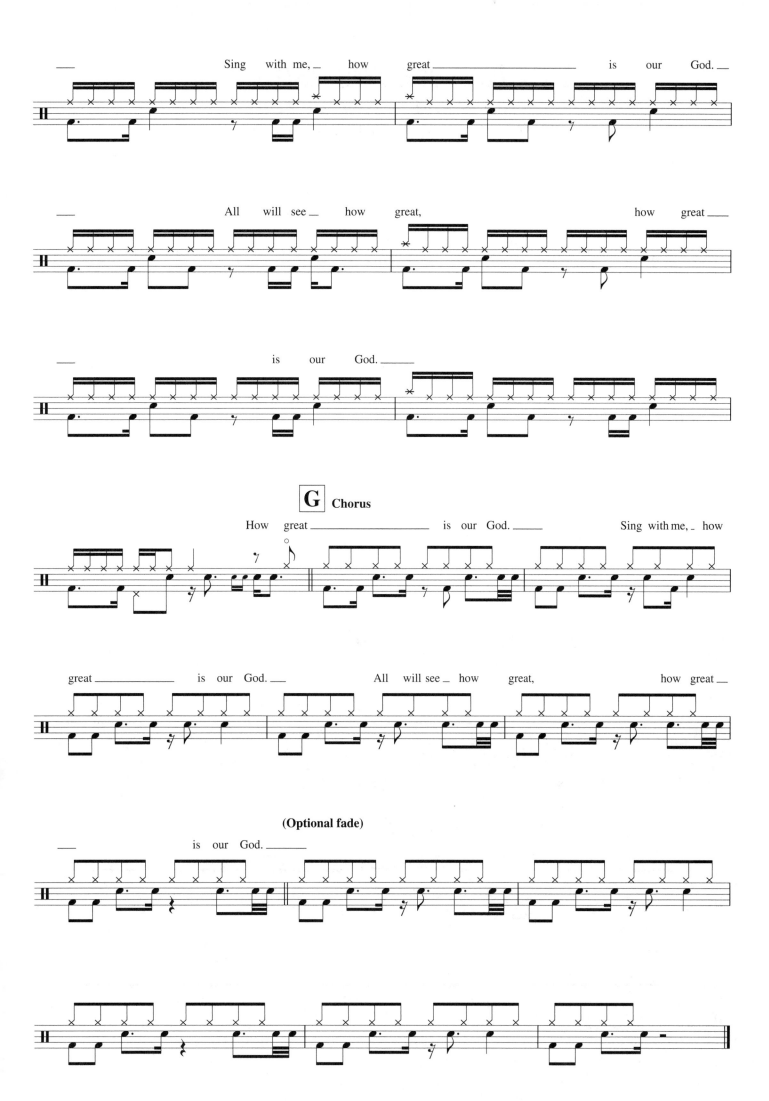

Let My Words Be Few
(I'll Stand in Awe of You)
Words and Music by Matt Redman and Beth Redman

No One Like You

Words and Music by Jack Parker, Mike Dodson, Jason Solley, Mike Hogan, Jeremy Bush and David Crowder

ev - er de - ny   the love of my   Sav - ior?

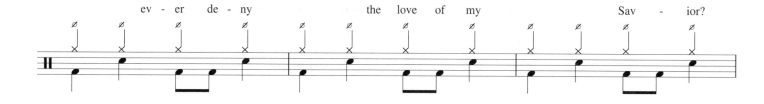

You are to me   ev - 'ry - thing,   all I need

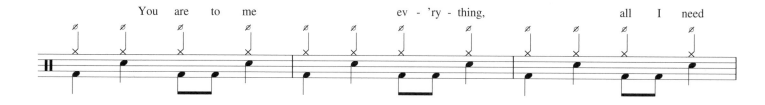

for - ev - er.   How   could   You

be   so   good?   There

B Chorus

is   no   one   like   You.

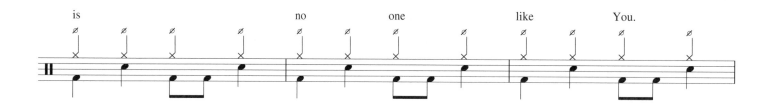

There   has   nev - er   ev - er   been

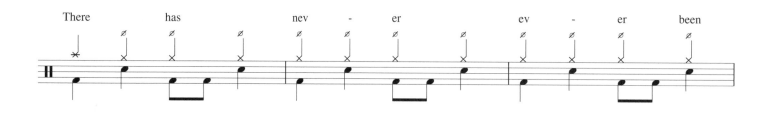

an - y - one   like   You.   **Interlude**

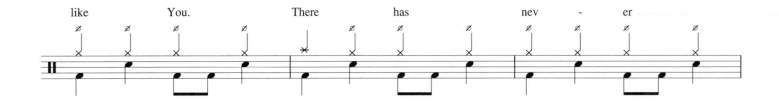

like   You.   There   has   nev - er

Chorus

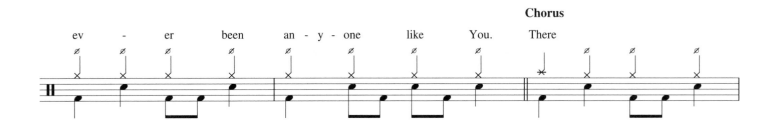

ev - er   been   an - y - one   like   You.   There

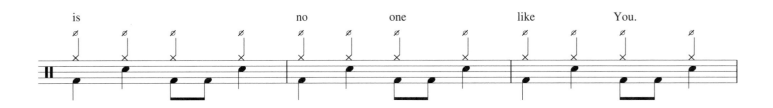

is   no   one   like   You.

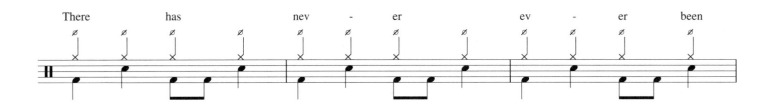

There   has   nev - er   ev - er   been

Interlude

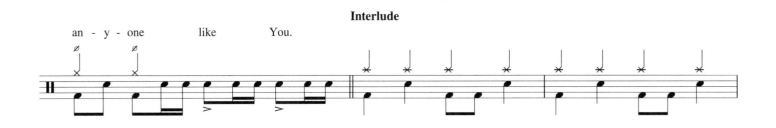

an - y - one   like   You.

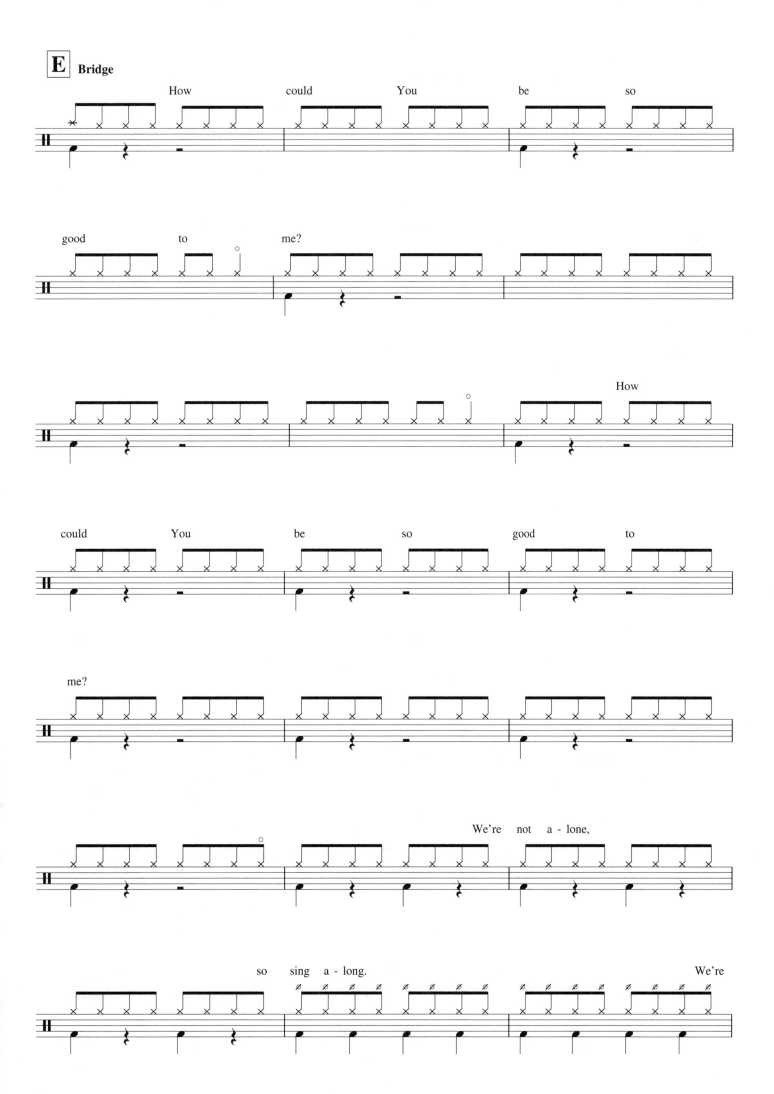

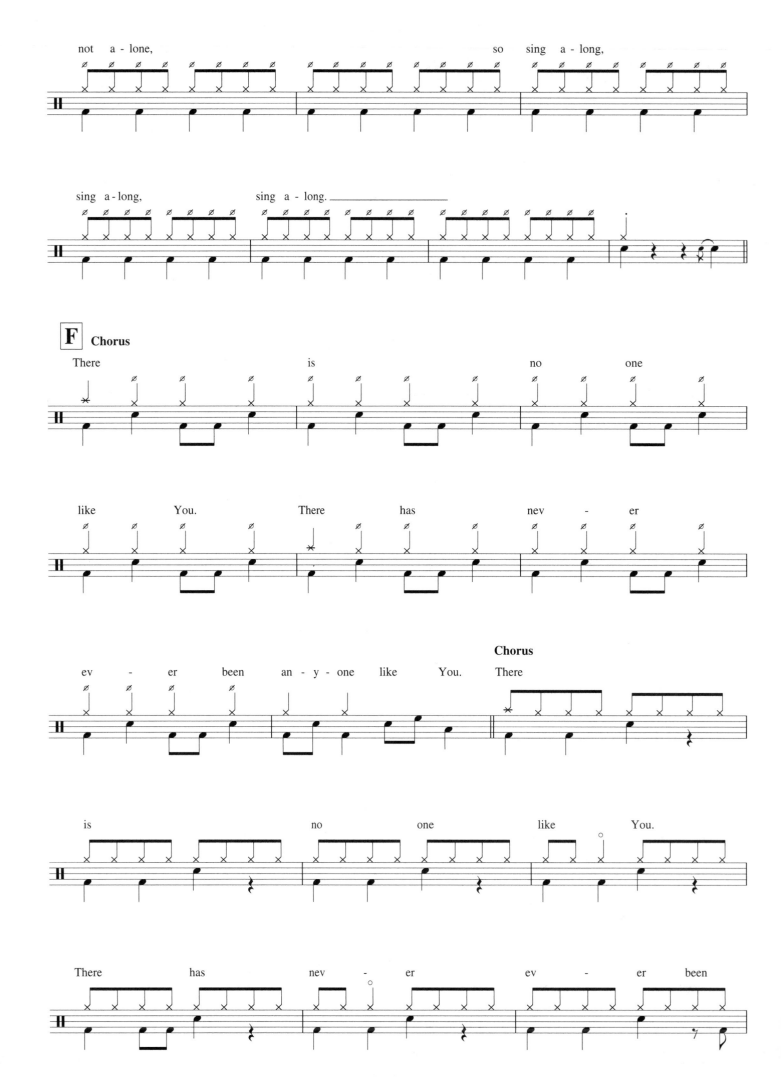

G Chorus

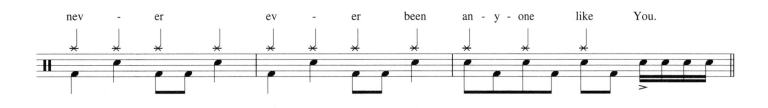

Chorus

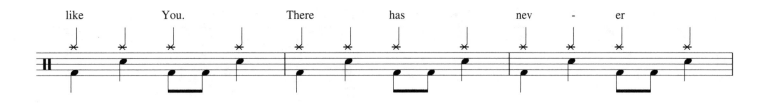

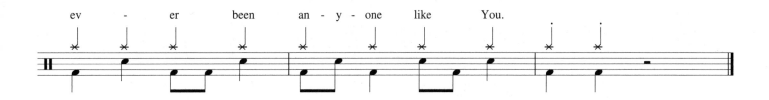

Wonderful Maker

Words and Music by Matt Redman and Chris Tomlin

13/14

Moderately slow (♩ = 78)
Intro

A **Verse 1**

You spread out the skies o - ver emp - ty space,

said, "Let there be light;" to a dark and form - less world Your light was born.

B **Verse 2**

You spread out Your arms o - ver emp - ty hearts,

said, "Let there be light;" to a dark and hope - less world Your Son was born.

C **Pre-Chorus**

You made the world and saw that it was_ good. You

Yesterday, Today and Forever

Words and Music by Vicky Beeching

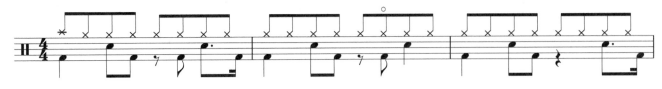

Moderately fast (♩ = 114)
Intro

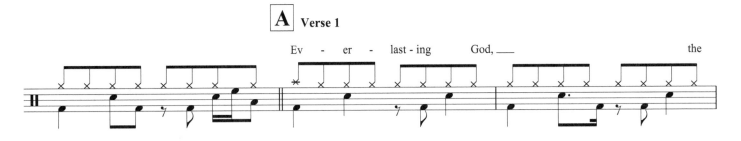

A Verse 1

Ev - er - last - ing God, ___ the

years go by, but You're ___ un - chang - ing. In this frag - ile world, ___

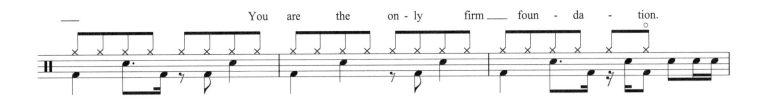

___ You are the on - ly firm ___ foun - da - tion.

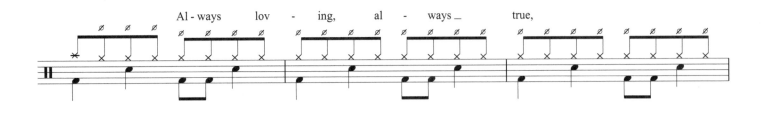

Al - ways lov - ing, al - ways ___ true,

al - ways mer - ci - ful ___ and good, ___

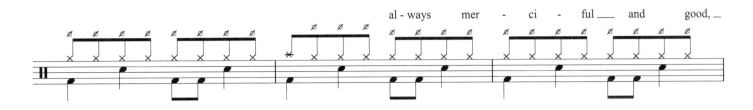

so ___ good. _____ Yes - ter - day, ___ to - day ___

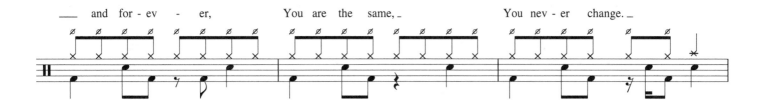

___ and for - ev - er, You are the same, ___ You nev - er change. ___

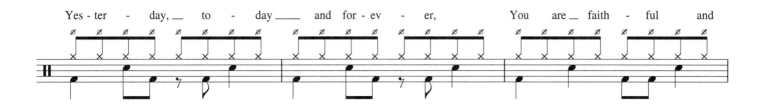

Yes - ter - day, ___ to - day ___ and for - ev - er, You are ___ faith - ful and

we will trust in ___ You. ___ We will trust ___ in You. ___

C Verse 2

Un - cre - at - ed One, ___

___ You have no end and no ___ be - gin - ning.

Earth - ly pow - ers fade, ___ but there is no end to ___

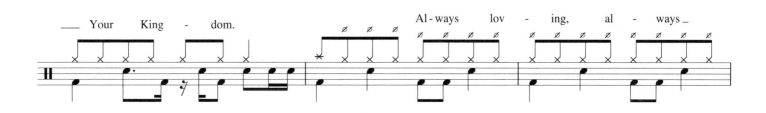

___ Your King - dom. Al - ways lov - ing, al - ways ___

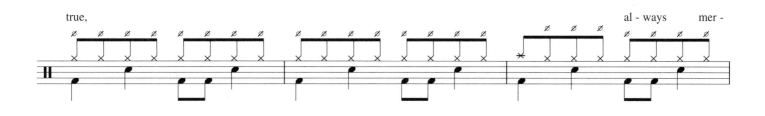

true, al - ways mer -

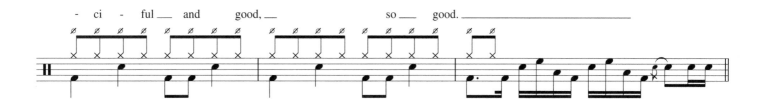

- ci - ful ___ and good, ___ so ___ good. _____

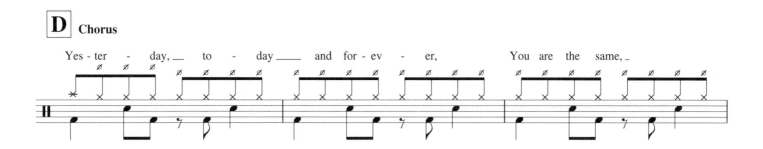

D Chorus

Yes - ter - day, ___ to - day ___ and for - ev - er, You are the same, __

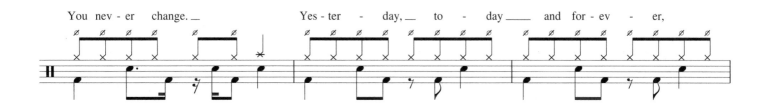

You nev - er change. ___ Yes - ter - day, ___ to - day ___ and for - ev - er,

You are _ faith - ful and we will trust in _ You. Yes - ter - day, _ to - day _

_ and for - ev - er, You are the same, _ You nev - er change. _

Yes - ter - day, _ to - day _ and for - ev - er, You are _ faith - ful and

F Interlude

we will trust in _ You. _ We will trust _ in _

_ You. We'll trust _ in You, _

in _ You. _

ABOVE ALL
PAUL BALOCHE and LENNY LeBLANC

Key of **G Major, 4/4**

INTRO:

G   G/B   C   D   Em7   D   C   Dsus   D

VERSE:

            C   Dsus   G
Above all powers,   above all kings
              C   Dsus   G
Above all nature and all created things
              Em   G/D   C   G/B
Above all wisdom and all the ways of man
Am7   Dsus   D
You were here before the world began
             C   Dsus   G
Above all kingdoms,   above all thrones
              C   Dsus   G
Above all wonders the world has ever known
              Em   G/D   C   G/B
Above all wealth and treasures of the earth
Am7   B7
There's no way to measure what You're worth

CHORUS:

G   Am7   D   G
Crucified,   laid behind a stone
          G   Am7   D   G
You lived to die   rejected and alone
             Em   G/D   C   G/B
Like a rose trampled on the ground
                Am7   G/B   C   Dsus
You took the fall   and thought of me
          G   G/B   C   Dsus   D
Above all (C/E D/F♯)

(REPEAT VERSE)

(REPEAT CHORUS 2X)

TAG:

D/F♯   Em   G/D   C   G/B
Like a rose trampled on the ground
                Am7   G/B   C   Dsus
You took the fall   and thought of me
          G   G/B   C   Dsus   D   G (hold)
Above all

BEAUTIFUL SAVIOR (ALL MY DAYS)

STUART TOWNEND

Key of **D Major**, 6/8

INTRO (2X):

Bm7   C6/9   D (2 bars)

VERSE 1:

Bm7   C6/9   D   G/B   C6/9   G
All my days I will sing this song of glad - ness

Bm7   C6/9   D   G/B Csus2
Give my praise to the Fountain of delights

  Am7 Csus2   D   Csus2 G/B   D
For in   my   helplessness, You heard   my   cry

    Am7   Csus2   Bm7   E/G♯   A
And waves   of   mercy poured down on my life

VERSE 2:

Bm7 C6/9   D   G/B   C6/9   G
I will trust in the cross of my Re - deem - er

Bm7 C6/9   D   G/B Csus2
I will sing of the blood that never fails

  Am7 Csus2 D   Csus2 G/B   D
Of sins   for - giv - en, of conscience cleansed

    Am7 Csus2   Bm7   A/C♯ Bm7 A
Of death   de -   feated and life without end

CHORUS:

A/G   D/F♯ G   A   A/C♯   D
Beautiful Savior,   Wonderful Coun - sel - or

      Em7   Em7/D
Clothed in majesty, Lord of history

      A/C♯   Bm7   A
You're the Way, the Truth, the Life

A/G   D/F♯   G   A A/C♯   D
Star of the Morning,   glorious in ho - li - ness

      Em7   Em7/D
You're the Risen One, heaven's champion

      A/C♯ Bm7 A   Bm7   C6/9   D (2 bars)
And You reign, You reign (over all)

VERSE 3:

 Bm7   C6/9   D   G/B C6/9   G
I long to be where the praise is never-end - ing

Bm7   C6/9   D   G/B Csus2
Yearn to dwell where the glory never fades

    Am7   Csus2 D   Csus2 G/B   D
Where count - less   worshippers will share   one   song

   Am7 Csus2 Bm7   A/C♯ Bm7 A
And cries   of   "Worthy!" will honor the Lamb

(REPEAT CHORUS 2X)

TAG:

Bm7   C6/9   D (2 bars)
(Vocal ad lib.)

DAYS OF ELIJAH

ROBIN MARK

Key of **G Major, 4/4**

INTRO (2X):

G C G D

VERSE 1:

```
G                    C     G       D       G
These are the days of Elijah, declaring the word of the Lord
    G                       C          G      D    G
And these are the days of Your servant Moses, righteousness being restored
    Bm                          Em     Am        C           Dsus   D
And though these are days of great trials, of famine and darkness and sword
    G                    C          G        D         G
Still we are the voice in the desert crying, "Prepare ye the way of the Lord!"
```

CHORUS:

```
    D        G                    C
Behold, He comes, riding on the clouds
             G                D
Shining like the sun at the trumpet call
        G               C
Lift your voice, it's the year of Jubilee
                    G    D    G    (C  G   D)
And out of Zion's hill salvation comes
```

VERSE 2:

```
    G                     C       G       D      G
And these are the days of Ezekiel, the dry bones becoming as flesh
    G                     C          G      D    G
And these are the days of Your servant David, rebuilding a temple of praise
    Bm                     Em     Am        C           Dsus   D
And these are the days of the harvest, the fields are as white in Your world
    G                    C          G       D       G
And we are the laborers in Your vineyard, declaring the word of the Lord
```

(REPEAT CHORUS 3X)

TAG:

```
D        G                    C
Lift your voice, it's the year of Jubilee
                    G    D    G (hold)
And out of Zion's hill salvation comes
```

HOW GREAT IS OUR GOD

CHRIS TOMLIN, JESSE REEVES and ED CASH

Key of **G Major, 4/4**

INTRO:

G (2 bars)

VERSE 1:

      G   **Em7**
The splendor of the King, clothed in majesty

                   Cmaj7
Let all the earth rejoice, all the earth rejoice

     G   **Em7**
He wraps Himself in light, and darkness tries to hide

                 Cmaj7
It trembles at His voice, trembles at His voice

CHORUS:

     G
How great is our God. Sing with me

    Em7
How great is our God. All will see

   Cmaj7   **D**   **G**
How great, how great is our God

VERSE 2:

G   **Em7**
Age to age He stands, and time is in His hands

             Cmaj7
Beginning and the End, Beginning and the End

     G   **Em7**
The God-head, Three in One, Father, Spirit, Son

          Cmaj7
The Lion and the Lamb, the Lion and the Lamb

(REPEAT CHORUS)

BRIDGE:

G   **Em7**
Name above all names, worthy of all praise

   Cmaj7   **D**   **G**
My heart will sing: How great is our God!

       G   **Em7**
He's the Name above all names, worthy of all praise

   Cmaj7   **D**   **G**
My heart will sing: How great is our God!

(REPEAT CHORUS 2X)

LET MY WORDS BE FEW (I'LL STAND IN AWE OF YOU)

MATT REDMAN and BETH REDMAN

Key of **G Major**, 4/4

INTRO:

G G+ Em7 Csus2

VERSE 1:

G   G+   Em7   Csus2
   You are God in heaven, and here am I on earth

G   G+   Em7   Csus2
   So I'll let my words be few

Am7 Em7 Csus2 D   G
Jesus, I am so   in love with You

CHORUS:

       G Fsus2 Em7 Am7 D7sus
And I'll stand in awe of You

       G Fsus2 Em7 Csus2
Yes, I'll stand in awe of You

    Am7   Em7   Csus2
And I'll let my words be few

Am7 Em7 Csus2 D   (G)
Jesus, I am so   in love with You

VERSE 2:

G   G+   Em7   Csus2
   The simplest of all love songs I want to bring to You

G   G+   Em7   Csus2
   So I'll let my words be few

Am7 Em7 Csus2 D   G
Jesus, I am so   in love with You

(REPEAT CHORUS 2X)

TAG:

Am7 Em7   Csus2

Am7 Em7   Csus2 D
Jesus, I am so   in love with You

OUTRO:

G G+   Em7 C D G (hold)

NO ONE LIKE YOU

JACK PARKER, MIKE DODSON, JASON SOLLEY, MIKE HOGAN, JEREMY BUSH and DAVID CROWDER

Key of **G Major, 4/4**

INTRO (2X):

G   D   Em7   Csus2

VERSE 1:

G   Em7   Dsus   Csus2
   You are more   beautiful   than anyone   ever

G   Em7   Dsus   Csus2
   And ev'ry day   You're the same,   You never change,   no, never

G   Em7   Dsus   Csus2
   And how could I   ever deny   the love of my   Savior?

G   Em7   Dsus   Csus2
   You are to me   ev'rything,   all I need   forever

D   C
   How could You be so good?

CHORUS:

G   D Em7 Csus2
There is   no one like You

G   D Em7   Csus2
There has never ever been anyone like You

INTERLUDE (2X):

G   D   Em7   Csus2

VERSE 2:

G   Em7   Dsus   Csus2
   Ev'rywhere,   You are there,   earth or air,   surrounding

G   Em7   Dsus   Csus2
   I'm not alone,   the heavens sing along.   My God, You're so   astounding

G   Em7   Dsus   Csus2
   How could You be   so good to me?   Eternally, I believe

(REPEAT CHORUS 2X)

(REPEAT INTERLUDE)

BRIDGE:

Dsus   Csus2   Dsus   Csus2
   How could You be so good to me?

Dsus   Csus2   Dsus   Csus2
   How could You be so good to me?

Dsus   Csus2
   We're not alone,   so sing along

Dsus   Csus2
   We're not alone,   so sing along, sing along, sing along

(REPEAT CHORUS 4X)

END ON G

WONDERFUL MAKER

MATT REDMAN and CHRIS TOMLIN

Key of **G Major, 4/4**

INTRO:

G/B C(add2)   Em7   G/B

VERSE 1:

C(add2)
You spread out the skies over empty space

Em7   C(add2)   D/F♯   G/B
Said, "Let there be light;" to a dark and formless world Your light was born

VERSE 2:

C(add2)
You spread out Your arms over empty hearts

Em7   C(add2)   D
Said, "Let there be light;" to a dark and hopeless world Your Son was born

PRE-CHORUS:

　　Am7   G/B   C(add2)
You made the world and saw that it was good

　　Am7   G/B   C(add2)   D/F♯
You sent Your only Son, for You are good

CHORUS:

　　　　　　　C(add2)   Em7
What a wonderful Maker, what a wonderful Savior

　　　　　　　C(add2)   D   G
How majestic Your whispers,   and how humble Your love

　　　　　　　C(add2)   Em7
With a strength like no other, and the heart of a Father

　　　　　　C(add2)   D   G
How majestic Your whispers,   what a wonderful God

VERSE 3:

　　　C(add2)
No eye has fully seen how beautiful the cross

　　Em7   C(add2)   D
And we have only heard the faintest whispers of how great You are

(REPEAT PRE-CHORUS)

(REPEAT CHORUS 2X)

TAG:

(G)   C(add2)   D   C(add2)   G (hold)
How majestic Your whispers,   what a wonderful God

YESTERDAY, TODAY AND FOREVER

VICKY BEECHING

Key of **D Major**, 4/4

INTRO:

D/F♯ G   Bm7 A

D/F♯ G   Bm7 A

VERSE 1:

G   Bm7
Everlasting God

    G   Bm7
The years go by, but You're unchanging

G   Bm7
In this fragile world

     G   Bm7
You are the only firm foundation

Em7   D/F♯
    Always loving, always true

G   Bm7   A
    Always merciful and good, so good

CHORUS:

D/F♯   G   Bm7   A
Yesterday, today and forever

D/F♯   G   Bm7   A
You are the same, You never change

D/F♯   G   Bm7   A
Yesterday, today and forever

Em7   G   A
You are faithful and we will trust in You

(REPEAT INTRO) – *Vocal ad lib.*

VERSE 2:

G   Bm7
Uncreated One

     G   Bm7
You have no end and no beginning

G   Bm7
Earthly powers fade

     G   Bm7
But there is no end to Your Kingdom

Em7   D/F♯
    Always loving, always true

G   Bm7   A
    Always merciful and good, so good

(REPEAT CHORUS 2X)

INTERLUDE:

G   D/F♯   G   D/F♯
(Vocal ad lib.)

BRIDGE:

G   D/F♯
Yahweh, God unchanging

G   D/F♯
Yahweh, firm foundation. You are

G   D/F♯
Yahweh, God unchanging

G   D/F♯
Yahweh, firm foundation

(REPEAT CHORUS 2X)

OUTRO (4X):

D/F♯ G   Bm7 A
(Vocal ad lib.)

END ON D

Worship Band Play-Along

The **Worship Band Play-Along** series is a flexible tool for worship leaders and bands. Each volume offers five separate, correlated book/CD packs: Guitar, Keyboard, Bass, Drumset, and Vocal. Bands can use the printed music and chord charts to play live together, and members can rehearse at home with the CD tracks. Worship leaders without a band can play/sing along with the CD for a fuller sound. The eight songs in each volume follow a similar theme for easy set selection, and the straightforward arrangements are perfect for bands of any level.

1. Holy Is the Lord

Includes: Agnus Dei • Be Unto Your Name • God of Wonders • Holy Is the Lord • It Is You • Open the Eyes of My Heart • We Fall Down • You Are Holy (Prince of Peace).

08740302	Vocal	$12.95
08740333	Keyboard	$12.95
08740334	Guitar	$12.95
08740335	Bass	$12.95
08740336	Drumset	$12.95

2. Here I Am to Worship

Includes: Come, Now Is the Time to Worship • Give Us Clean Hands • Hear Our Praises • Here I Am to Worship • I Give You My Heart • Let Everything That Has Breath • You Alone • You're Worthy of My Praise.

08740337	Vocal	$12.95
08740338	Keyboard	$12.95
08740409	Guitar	$12.95
08740441	Bass	$12.95
08740444	Drumset	$12.95

3. How Great Is Our God

Includes: Above All • Beautiful Savior (All My Days) • Days of Elijah • How Great Is Our God • Let My Words Be Few (I'll Stand in Awe of You) • No One Like You • Wonderful Maker • Yesterday, Today and Forever.

08740540	Vocal	$12.95
08740571	Keyboard	$12.95
08740572	Guitar	$12.95
08740608	Bass	$12.95
08740635	Drumset	$12.95

COMING SOON!

4. He Is Exalted

Includes: Beautiful One • God of All • He Is Exalted • In Christ Alone • Lord Most High • Lord, Reign in Me • We Want to See Jesus Lifted High • Worthy Is the Lamb.

08740646	Vocal	$12.95
08740651	Keyboard	$12.95
08740712	Guitar	$12.95
08740741	Bass	$12.95
08745665	Drumset	$12.95

FOR MORE INFORMATION, SEE YOUR LOCAL MUSIC DEALER, OR WRITE TO:

HAL•LEONARD® CORPORATION

7777 W. BLUEMOUND RD. P.O. BOX 13819 MILWAUKEE, WI 53213

www.halleonard.com

Prices, contents, and availability subject to change without notice.